Faust (Faust is Dead)

Faust (Faust is Dead)
'. . . an intelligent and witty reappropriation of the legend . . .
alive, pertinent and disturbing.'
Michael Coveney, *The Observer*

The world's most famous philosopher arrives in Los Angeles
and is greeted as a star. In a round of chat show appearances,
he announces the Death of Man and the End of History.
When he meets up with a young man who is on the run from
his father, a leading software magnate, they embark on a
hedonistic voyage across America. But in the play's bloody
conclusion, they discover that not all events are virtual.

Mark Ravenhill trained at Bristol University. Theatre
writing includes *Shopping and Fucking* for Out of Joint and the
Royal Court Theatre, 1996 and *Faust* for Actors' Touring
Company, 1997. He is currently the Literary Director at
Paines Plough.

D1102987

also available:

Shopping and Fucking

for a complete catalogue of Methuen Drama titles write to:

Methuen Drama
Random House
20 Vauxhall Bridge Road
London SW1V 2SA

FAUST (FAUST IS DEAD)

Mark Ravenhill

Methuen Drama

First published 1997

© Mark Ravenhill 1997

Mark Ravenhill has asserted his right
under the Copyright, Designs and Patents Act 1988
to be identified as the author of this work

First published in the United Kingdom in 1997 by Methuen
Random House, 20 Vauxhall Bridge Road,
London SW1V 2SA

Random House Australia (Pty) Limited
20 Alfred Street, Milsons Point, Sydney,
New South Wales 2061, Australia

Random House New Zealand Limited
18 Poland Road, Glenfield,
Auckland 10, New Zealand

Random House South Africa (Pty) Limited
Endulini, 5A Jubilee Road, Parktown 2193, South Africa

Random House UK Limited Reg. No. 954009

A CIP catalogue record for this book is available from the
British Library
ISBN 0 413 71840 9

Typeset by Wilmaset Ltd., Birkenhead, Wirral
Printed and bound in Great Britain
by Athenaeum Press Ltd, Gateshead, Tyne & Wear

Caution

All rights in this version are strictly reserved and
applications for performance etc. should be made to the
author's agent: Casarotto Ramsay Ltd, National House,
60–66 Wardour Street, London W1V 4ND. No performance
may be given unless a licence has been obtained.

Faust (Faust is Dead)

A Note on the Text

All plays are outlines, waiting for actors, directors and
designers to make them three-dimensional, but this one is
written to allow particular space for their creative talents
and therefore needs a particular act of imagination on the
part of a reader.

   The play was the outcome of a week's workshop with
Actors' Touring Company and continued to develop during
a further workshop, the rehearsal period and through
preview performances. The original production made use of
video sequences, the physical skills of the performers, music
and light.

   I would like to dedicate the play to Nick Philippou, the
director, Hetty Shand, the producer and Alain Pelletier and
Pete Bailey, the actors. Although all the words in the finished
play are mine, their imaginations and opinions all shaped the
writing of *Faust*.

A slash in the dialogue (/) indicates that the next actor
should start their line, creating overlapping speech.

Mark Ravenhill, 1997

Faust (Faust is Dead) was commissioned and first produced by Actors' Touring Company for a national tour in 1997. The cast was as follows:

Alain	Alain Pelletier
Pete	Pete Bailey
Donny	Andy Broadhurst
Chorus	Students from Marymount College

Directed by Nick Philippou
Produced by Hetty Shand
Designed by Pippa Nissen
Lighting by Zerlina Hughes
Music by Neil Starr
Video by Alan Pelletier

Characters

Alain, *French*
Pete, *American*
Donny
Chorus

Setting: The West Coast of America. Present Day.

Scene One

Chorus   See, a few years ago I couldn't sleep. I'd go to bed and then I got thinking about all this stuff in the world – about the riots and the fighting and all the angry people and all – and I just couldn't sleep. And sometimes I'd cry – partly because I really wanted to sleep and I was mad that I couldn't sleep, but partly because of all those bad things going on. And my mom would come into my room and be just like so totally freaked that I was crying night after night. 'What's wrong, poops? You have to tell me what's wrong. Is it the teachers at the school? Is one of the teachers at the school doing bad things to you?'
Until eventually I'm like:
'No, mom, it's not the teachers at the school. I'm crying for the world, because the world is such a bad place.'
And momma is like:
'I know, poops. It's bad now but it's getting better. It's gonna get a whole lot better. We're going to live in a better world.'
'I know, momma.'
And so I pretended to sleep and my mom went off to bed. And after that I taught myself to cry in a special way that meant she wouldn't hear me ever again.

Scene Two

TV show.

David Letterman   So . . . you're here, you're in America. And you've written a book. And you've called it *The Death of Man* . . .

Alain   Yes. That is correct. Yes.

David Letterman   Neat title. What exactly does it mean?

Alain   Well, it's a complex thing to explain in a few minutes.

David Letterman   Because I have to tell you, right now I feel pretty much alive.

Laughter.

Alain   Oh yes, of course.

David Letterman   And it seems to me that you seem pretty much alive as well.

Alain   Yes, but I'm talking about man as an idea.

David Letterman   Uh uh/uh huh, yeah, yeah.

Alain   As an idea, as a construct.

David Letterman   Madonna, have you read the book?

Madonna   Not yet, David.

David Letterman   But you're going to, right?

Madonna   I've been pretty busy David/you know that.

David Letterman   But you've read the other/stuff, right?

Madonna   Sure, sure. The book about sexuality I thought was great.

David Letterman   Now, that is a surprise.

Laughter.

Scene Three

Alain   I was invited to join the Director of Studies for a meal. Sushi, miso soup, sake. We were entertaining a potential sponsor for the department. He was a Japanese. And our potential sponsor asks me:
'What are you thinking about today? Please, I understand you do a lot of thinking and I'd like to know – what are you thinking about today?'
What am I thinking about today?
Well today, I am considering an example:
In 1981 a Dutch woman was on business in Tokyo, when she met a Japanese businessman. He invited her to join him for a

meal. She read him some of her poetry. While she was reading, he shot her. Several times. He then chopped her up, put her in his bowl and ate her.

That is what I am thinking about today.

The potential sponsor did not like the example. He was very angry.

And Ms Brannigan – the Director of Studies is called Ms Brannigan – Ms Brannigan was angry also.

I had never read the guidelines. It seems no discourse within the university should be in any way offensive to women or to any member of a religious or racial grouping.

Ms Brannigan said that of course the incident would only result in a warning, not a disciplinary action.

But it was the last of the straws. The camel's back was broken.

And I told Ms Brannigan to go fuck herself.

And I decided that maybe I should live a little.

Scene Four

Tatty apartment. Very late.

Alain *is sitting. Very drunk, or stoned, or something.* **Pete** *is standing.*

Pete   You wanna take your jacket off?
Take your jacket off. Relax.
See, you relax then I guess I might relax too. Okay?
Please. Allow me.

Pete *tries to remove the jacket.*

Come on. That's it. Come on.
I kind of know one of the guys, sorta know him a little, you know? And he said that you're A and R, that you're seeking to sign Stev and the band. To a major label.
You do have an . . . an . . . aura . . . of . . . authority.

Sings, grunge fashion –

Got a killer in my VCR
Killer in my ROM
Killer on the cable news
Killer in the floss I use
Killer in the floss
Killer in the floss
Killer in the floss

See? Neat words. No. Great words. Words, yeah but also
something about the way Stevie . . . like he really totally
means it, you know? Which is like, totally marketable. And I
am telling you that Stevie and the band are like totally the
thing.
Just beer. That all? Is that what you're saying to me – you get
like this with beer?
If it's beer I can taste it, okay?

Pete *kisses* **Alain**.

You wanna stay over? Stay over if you want.
Yeah. This a box. Or a hole. Both a box and a hole.
This is good. To talk with you like this is good. It's
interesting. For me. Because you're different . . .

Pete *kisses* **Alain**.

Different can be sexy. Sometimes.
See, one of the guys figured that you were old and uncool
enough – no offence intended – old and uncool enough to be
A and R and Stevie sort of sent out word that if anyone was
like prepared to . . . please you then Stevie could be very
grateful to that person.
So, if you wanna . . .
Okay, I understand. Sleep it off. Why not?

Pete *tries to lift* **Alain** *up. Gives up.*

Goodnight.
'Killer in the floss
Killer in the floss
Killer in the floss'
We'll talk tomorrow about your signing of Stevie . . .

Alain (*in French*)   Because in America, and only in
America, am I truly at home.
For me, and for so many children of this twentieth century, it
is only in America that we really believe that we are alive,
that we are living within in our own century.

Pete   Look. Hold it right there.

Pete *fetches his camcorder*.

I'm sorry. I'm sorry but I only have a little . . . so you have to
go really slowly. Slowly. Okay.

Pete *videos* **Alain**.

Alain (*in French*)   Because in America,/ and only in
America, am I truly at home.
For me, and for so many children of this twentieth century, it
is only in America that we really believe that we are alive,
that we are living within our own century.
In Europe, we are ghosts, trapped in a museum, with the
lights out and the last visitor long gone.
And so I am going to America.

Pete   Because in America . . . just America . . . is . . . really
. . . home.
For me, and for children in the twentieth century (for kids?
what's the . . . ?) . . . it is only America (uh uh, uh, uh, uh uh)
. . . dah dah dah belief in being alive (right), living in the
century (century that we – what? – own).
In Europe, we are spooks (phantoms, ghosts, yeah),
something in a some . . . (shit, he's getting . . ., shit), lights off
and the somesuch something, yeah yeah yeah yeah.

Alain (*in French*)   And/ so I am going to America.

Pete   And so I am going to America.

Alain (*in French*)   And so I say:
(*In American English.*) Hi America. How ya doin'?

Pete   Hi Europe. America's doing . . . just fine.
America's . . . yeah.

Scene Five

Chorus   Yeah, I know Stevie a little. My friend Jose swears
Stevie worked my shift at the drive-through a few years back
and Jose says that maybe Stevie and I even shared the same
overalls. Which is amazing. Although Jose does lie from time
to time.
See, when I look at Stevie and Stevie is up there singing,
sometimes I see . . . I know this may sound way pretentious or
way dumb or whatever . . . but look at Stevie and I see Kurt.
It is like Kurt's . . . spirit . . . yeah, yeah teen spirit if you will
. . . that his spirit is coming back to us through Stevie . . . who
is just beautiful, okay? In a negative sort of a way.

Scene Six

The next morning.

Alain *asleep in the chair. Enter* **Pete** *with junkfood breakfast.*

Pete   You wanna eat?
Hey guy, you wanna eat something?
Good for you to eat something.
Here. Here. Okay. For you.

Alain   Thank you.

Pete   You speak English?

Alain   Of course.

Pete   Okay, that's cool.
It's just . . . last night . . .
You remember last night?

Alain   Oh yes.

Pete   Okay.
And did you find the sex good?
Did you find our sexual contact a worthwhile and
stimulating experience?

Alain   Yes.

Pete   Yes, the sex was good?

Alain   Yes. The sex was good.

Pete   That's what I figured.
I figured you didn't remember a thing.
The sex was zero. There was zero sex.

Alain   Alright.

Pete   You talked good enough.
So, you're not A and R? Artists and Repertoire?

Alain   No. I'm sorry.

Pete   That's okay. That's what one of the guys ... totally dumb.
So why were you there?
You know one of the band?

Alain   The beer.

Pete   Okay.

Alain   The beer was good.

Pete   I understand.
But if you're not A and R you're gonna have to go.

Alain   I understand.

Alain *moves to exit, turns.*

Alain   What do you think about this?

Pete   I'm sorry.

Alain   I'd like you to consider this example. I want to know what you think.
A man meets a woman.
And he takes this woman home to his apartment and he makes love to this woman.

Pete   This is a story?

Alain   An example.

Pete   Okay. An example.

Alain   They are making love and she asks him a question.
Which is:
Which part of me do you find the most . . . the most . . .

Pete   The most arousing?

Alain   Attractive. Which part of me do you find the most
attractive?
And he replies: the eyes.
It is the eyes he finds the most attractive part of this woman.

Pete   Okay.

Alain   So, the next morning he leaves. He works. But all the
time he is thinking about this beautiful woman, about
making love with this beautiful woman, yes?

Pete   Yes. He's thinking about her.

Alain   The following day, he is woken by the front
doorbell. The doorbell is ringing, so he jumps out of bed. It
might be her. Maybe she can't bear to be apart from him.

Pete   Maybe she feels the same way too.

Alain   Exactly.
But it isn't her. It's the mailman. Who has a parcel for him.
So he signs for the parcel and he takes the parcel into the
kitchen and he realises that the parcel . . . smells.

Pete   Of her?

Alain   Yes.

Pete   The parcel has the woman's smell.

Alain   His hands are trembling with excitement as he pulls
away the packaging – he wants the moment to last, but also
he wants to discover the contents.
And as the packaging falls away, a box is revealed. A
cardboard box, (*Indicates.*) so big . . .

Pete   Like a shoe-box?

Alain   The sort of box in which you might buy shoes. The
sort of cardboard box that has a lid on it.
The lid is on. He waits for a moment, delaying the moment of

pleasure and then he lifts up the lid.
And inside the box are two human eyes.

Pete   So, she'd . . . Right.
She'd cut out her eyes.

Alain   Exactly. She had cut out her eyes.
Which leaves us with a question. This example gives rise to
an important question.
Who was the seducer and who was the seduced?

Pete   The woman with no eyes and the guy with two
eyeballs in a box. One's the seducer, one's been seduced.

Alain   Precisely.

Pete   And which one is which?
Well, that's an interesting question.

Alain   You think so?

Pete   Yeah. I think that's a very interesting question.
You think a lot about that kind of stuff?

Alain   Oh yes.

Pete   That is cool.
I think about that kind of stuff.
You wanna tell me a little about yourself?
Tell me about the guy who thinks about all that.

Alain *moves to kiss* **Pete**.

Pete   No.
It's okay.
It's not like I have a prejudice or, or a problem you know . . .
with the whole guys thing. It's just, like, it's not totally me,
okay? Sure if you were gonna sign Stevie, but otherwise . . .

Alain   I understand.

Alain *moves to leave.*

Pete   . . . How did she find the mailbox?

Alain   I'm sorry?

Pete That's my question.

She's there in her apartment, she's taken out her eyes, say a
pair of nail scissors, something like that. So, okay, she's laid
everything out in front of her. The shoe-box, the paper, the
sellotape. And I guess she's, like, written the address on
before she's become . . . visually impaired. So, it's all within
easy reach.

But that still begs the question:

How did she find the mailbox?

Alain That is not relevant.

It is an example, a model. The details are not relevant.

Pete The mailbox is a detail, right?

Alain Yes. Just so. The mailbox is a detail.

Pause.

Pete I don't want you to go, okay?

I want you to stay here.

You stay here, but I'd just feel better if you didn't do the
kissing thing, okay?

I prefer it this way.

And see if you wanna bring anyone else back, I can do
watching, I can do recording. I just don't do doing, okay?
Deal?

Alain She was blind. The woman was blind.

Pete Well, sure. She'd cut out her eyes.

Alain But you said 'visually impaired'. She was blind.

Pete Okay, yes. She was blind.

Alain Yes. I stay. It's a deal.

Scene Seven

Chorus It's happening just like they said. Whole city's
blowing right apart.

Some guy smashed the window of the store and so I got

myself a VCR. Latest model. Just reached in there and got myself that honey. Bit a glass in my thumb's all the suffering I had.

'Cept I get this bitch home and my momma she's like: 'A VCR? You bring me a VCR? When we ain't got no food in the kitchen? You coulda done the food store. Listen to God, he would have told you – go do the food store.'

And I'm like: 'Momma, what is the point of food in the house when you have nothing to watch while you're eating it?'

Scene Eight

Alain *is lying on the floor, blood on his face. Enter* **Pete**, *with his camcorder.*

Pete   'What is the point of food in the house when you have nothing to watch while you're eating it.'

Got it all on tape. Guys looting shops, guys burning cars, guys burning guys.

Oh jesus.

Come on guy. Come on.

What has happened to you?

Alain (*in French*)   In 1981 a Dutch woman was on business in Tokyo/ when she met a Japanese businessman.

Pete   No, come on. Please. You have to . . . in English, okay?

Here . . . you have to . . . calm.

What happened?

Alain (*in English*)   . . . In 1981, in Toyko, a Dutch woman was on business. On business in Tokyo and she met a man, a Japanese man. Through her business. They became friendly, their friendship grew until eventually she ate dinner with him.

Pete   / Okay, I don't see the rel . . . okay.

Alain   They are eating and she reveals, she tells him that she is a poet. She writes poetry. Love poetry. She has a poem

about him and would he like to hear the poem?
Well, alright.
So he's eating and she starts to read the poem and he pulls out
a gun and he shoots her. He shoots her dead. And then he eats
her. Cuts her up and puts her in his bowl and he eats her, and
as he's eating her, all the time he's declaring his love for her.
His undying love.
Who was cruel? The man or the woman?

Pete　Please. I don't get it. I'm not so good at the whole
metaphor thing.
So you have to . . . the blood is real.

Alain　It's boring.

Pete　That's okay.

Alain　It's just a thing . . .
It's a foolish thing.

Pete　That is cool.
No really.
So . . .

Alain　Just a guy, you know. Okay. Guy in a bar.
Says that he likes me.
Says that I don't say a lot of words.
And please, it is so exciting the way I look and don't talk
and of course he has a place, or he has a place and it's just not
the right place for him just now, so maybe if I knew of some
place . . .

Pete　Any time you want to do that, you do that, it's cool.
You know that.

Alain　So we got here and then he attacks me.
Attacks my eyes.

Pete　Oh Jesus.

Alain　Goes for my eyes.
Until they are full with blood. My blood.
And I don't know what . . .

Pete　You got to be careful, you know that?

Alain   'This one is for Bill'.

Pete   I'm sorry?

Alain   He says to me.
I'm down and I'm bleeding and he says to me:
'This one is for Bill'.

Pete   Shit.

Alain   Please, what does this . . . ?

Pete   Fucking Jesus fucking . . .
No.
You . . . arsehole fuck.

Alain   Yes. What does that . . . ?
This one is for Bill.
Does that mean something?

Pete   Well, yes, yes of course.
Of course that means something.

Alain   You know what this means?

Pete   Oh yeah.
Oh yeah. I know what that means.

Alain   So. Please . . .

Pete   Jesus, how could you . . . ?
How could you do this to me?
Have you no control?
What is it with you faggots that you can't fucking . . . I mean,
can't you wait or something? Ask questions maybe?
Well, fuck you.

Pete *exits and then re-enters with a floppy disc.*

Well, that's okay then. Oh thank God. Praise be.
I'm sorry. I'm sorry.
You better come with me.
Come on. Get your shit together.

Alain   You want to go . . . ?

Pete   I'm getting out of here.
We're getting out of here.
Come on. Come on.

Pete *starts to gather together his stuff.*

Look. He's gonna come back, okay? They're not gonna let
this lie, you know?
See this (*the disc*)? Guy who attacked you was looking for this.
This is chaos.
Only copy in the world.
See, my dad's seen the future and he knows how to give his
product the lead for, like, centuries into the new millennium.
Chaos is the answer.
My dad sets up his team. Hundreds of guys looking for that
nudge into chaos.
And one day, they are there. It's ready to be released onto
the market.
Except I hate my dad so bad and I download a virus in the
chaos programme. Total meltdown.
So all he has now is shit.
And it's just me with the real thing.
Which means he hates me but also he wants to find me real
bad, you know?
So. Please.

Alain   I like this place.

Pete   Because my dad wants to be everywhere. His
software in every home, on every desk. Bill, Bill, Bill. Like
God, God, God.

Alain   Bill is your father?

Pete   Yeah. Bill's my dad.
I hate my dad.
You coming with me?

Scene Nine

Car driving through the city.

Alain Where are we going?

Pete Dunno.

Alain We're just going to ...

Pete Yeah, just gonna drive.
That bother you?

Alain No. That's okay.

Pete Just gonna drive and drive.
If we anticipate even a little then my dad could figure out where to find us.
My dad sees the future like a journey down a long road.
I'm like: dad, you sure there's gonna be a future?
You wanna tell me a little about yourself?

Alain No.

Pete When you talk, you talk very well.

Long pause.

Alain I want to fuck you.

Pete Yeah?

Alain I need to fuck you. Or you fuck me.

Pete Maybe. Okay.
I don't have a problem with that.

Alain You want me to get out of the car?

Pete No. I want you here with me.

Alain You can stop the car and let me out.

Pete No. I don't want to do that.

Alain If I stay with you, I fuck you.
We drive somewhere. We drive to the desert and I fuck you.

Pete Sure, sure, I understand.
If that's the deal ...

Alain   That's the deal.

Pete   Then I guess I'll learn to handle that.

Alain   Good.

Pete   So. You're attracted to me right?
I'm gonna be rich. Is that what you're thinking?
See, time will pass and my dad will need this (*the disc*) so bad
and then I'm gonna offer it back for a sum so vast.
And then I'm gonna buy so many totally real experiences.
I'm gonna work alongside Mother Theresa. I'm gonna take
Saddam Hussein out for a pizza. I'm gonna shoot pool with
the Pope and have Boris Yeltsin show me his collection of
baseball stickers.
So who are you?

Alain   I am the man who is going to fuck you.

Pete   Yes. I see that.

Scene Ten

Desert. Night.

Alain   This is beautiful.

Pete   You like it?

Alain   Oh yes.
This is a very beautiful place.

Pete   I guess it's okay.
I kind of prefer it on the TV.
I prefer it with a frame around it, you know?

Alain   Okay.

Pete   Like you know, it stretches out, there it goes, on and
on – you get the point from the TV – but when you actually
see it, you know . . . it's a little scary.
Excuse me, I'm gonna have to . . .

Pete *takes out the camcorder, looks through it.*

That's better.
I kind of feel okay now.
This always works for me. Some guys it's Prozac, but with me . . .

Alain   I understand.

Alain *starts to feel* **Pete**'s *genitals.*

Pete   Oh god.
You faggot scum.

Alain   Yes.
That's it.
That's okay.

Pete   I don't have a prejudice here.
You filthy little weenie-feeling heap of shit.
I believe in Positive Action.
I believe in the multiplicity of sexualities within our society.

Alain   If you look through . . .

Pete   Sure, sure.

Alain   If you continue to look through . . .

Pete   Yes. Yes.

Alain   Keep it all within the frame.

Pete   You're right.
You're right.
I can do that.

Alain   It's on TV, okay?
It's something on TV.

Pete   Yes.

Pete *records* **Alain** *playing with his genitals.*

Alain   Is that okay?

Pete   Yeah. That's okay.

Alain *starts to suck* **Pete** *off.*

Pete (*TV commentary voice*)   Lost under the stars,
surrounded by the splendour of nature and the mysterious
awesomeness of Death Valley, the kid is initiated into the
strange world of the homosexual.

Alain   You don't have to speak.

Pete   I do.

Alain   Please. No.
You don't have to say anything.

Pete   I do. Okay. I do.
Make it like on TV, okay?
And I can do that, I really can do that.
But only if I have the commentary.
I need the voice.

Alain   No.

Pete   No?

Alain   I don't want you to do that voice.

Pete   Okay.

Alain *continues to suck* **Pete** *off for some time in silence.*

Pete   There goes a racoon . . . hoppity hopping through
that piece of tumbleweed.
I'm sorry.
I'm sorry.
Hoppity hop.
Quiet.
Stop it.
That commentator. He just keeps on going.
Hoppity hop. Hey little fella, how you doing?
And if that little fella could speak, he would tell us:
I'm doing just fine. I'm living life out here at one with
Mother Nature. Don't you just wish you could do the same?

Alain *turns away and spits* **Pete**'s *cum from his mouth.*

Pete   Did I come?

Alain   Yes.

Pete   Really?

Alain   Plenty.

Pete   Really, that is amazing. That is so cool.
Because you know something?
I didn't feel a thing.
You wanna go back to the car?

Alain   That's not the deal. I want to stay here.

Pete   You wanna stay here for the night?

Alain   We're gonna stay here for the night.

Pete   Alright. I'll try.

Pete *sits.*
Looks through camcorder.
Doesn't look through camcorder.

Here. Here. I have a supply.

Pete *brings out a stash of different pills.*

Here, you see. This is what we do. We go through this.
You wanna go through the nature thing?

Alain   Yes.

Pete   You wanna go through the Nature thing and you
wanna go through the Sex thing?

Alain   Yes. Both.

Pete   Okay.
So now we are going to have an experience. Which is fine.
But just by themselves, on their own, okay, experiences don't
have a shape.
They don't have a shape and they don't have a rhythm.
And without shape, without rhythm, the experience can be
too much, it can be too painful.
So we shape the experience.
Like this.

Pete *arranges the pills in a circle around them.*

Alain We don't have to decide the shape. We don't have to know in advance: this one will take me up, this one will take me down, this one will be spacy, this one will bring it all into focus.
Let's not do that.
We'll just do them at random and allow the shape to emerge. You understand?

Alain *closes his eyes, spins around, chooses a pill and takes it.*

Alain And now you.

They repeat the same process and **Pete** *takes a pill.*

Alain Do you know what you want?

Pete No.

Alain But you want to find out?

Pete Yeah. I wanna find out.

Alain I don't want any limits, you understand?

Pete I understand.

Alain And how does this make you feel?

Pete I don't know.

Alain Scared?

Pete Yes, scared. And, and . . .

Alain Excited?

Pete Excited also. Yes.

They kiss.

Alain Man is dead, you know.
And Progress. Progress also. Progress is dead.
And Humanity. Yes. Humanity is dead.

Pete So we're free, right?

Alain I'm going to fuck you.

Pete I know.
You feel anything yet?

Alain   Yes. I think it's starting.

Alain *fucks* **Pete**.

Scene Eleven

Motel Chalet. **Alain** *sits watching TV.*

Pete   I asked the guy.
I asked the guy and he said that he had plenty of other chalets.

Alain   Is that so?

Pete   Yeah. They have plenty of chalets.
You see that.
It's quiet around here, you know?

Alain   Better than the desert.

Pete   Better than the desert for that whole no people thing.
So if you wanted another chalet . . .

Alain   You think/ I should have another chalet?

Pete   Yeah. That's what I'm saying. If you wanted maybe, like, your own chalet.

Alain   I don't want my own chalet.
I'm fine. This is fine.

Pete   Yeah, but I think . . .
I think you should have your own chalet.

Alain   You do?

Pete   Wouldn't you like that?

Alain   No. I wouldn't like that.

Pete   You wouldn't like your own chalet?
It's what I'd like. I'd like for you to have your own chalet.

Alain   No.

Pete   Because . . . ?

Alain   Because I want to be with you.

Pete Because you want to be with me?
Fine, okay, but I don't want to be with you.
You see? You understand?
Okay, we had an experience. Fine. That's cool. Thank you.
There see, I'm grateful. We shared an experience, I did a lot
of new stuff. I was scared but we got through it . . . when were
there . . . great.
But that's over . . . I'm bored.

Alain Oh yes. Of course.

Pete We've done it now, haven't we?

Alain Then we'll find new things, new experiences.

Pete I don't want that. There's no danger.

Alain There's plenty of dangers.

Pete I don't want you in the bed.
You're creepy.

Alain Fine.
I'll sleep on the floor.

Pete Is that what you want to do?

Alain That's what I'm going to do.

Pete I'm gonna sleep with this (*the disc*) from now on. This
is the only thing that is precious to me.

Alain I understand.

Scene Twelve

The next morning.

Pete I know you. I know who you are.

Alain Of course. Yes. You know everything.

Pete Last night. I was cruel. I'm sorry. But I didn't know
who you were.
This place sucks, you know? Sucks so bad they don't invest in
the proper channels. But what they do have is the kind of

channels that show re-runs of re-runs.
Like . . . re-runs of old chatshows, okay?

Pete *plays a video tape.*

> **David Letterman**   So . . . you're here, you're in
> America. And you've written a book. And you've called
> it *The Death of Man* . . .
>
> **Alain**   Yes. That is correct. Yes.
>
> **David Letterman**   Neat title. What exactly does it
> mean?
>
> **Alain**   Well, it's a complex thing to explain in a few
> minutes.
>
> **David Letterman**   Because I have to tell you, right
> now I feel pretty much alive.
>
> *Laughter.*

Pete *puts the video on hold.*

Pete   See. You see?
That's the way I know.
You gonna go back to the university? Now you lived a little.

Alain   No.

Pete   Because . . .

Alain   Because I . . . have . . . burnt my bridges.

Pete   You're so metaphorical.
What does that mean? On the TV show.
What does that mean – the End of History?
Please. I want to learn.
I want to be with you and I want you to teach me.

Alain   That means . . .

Pete *goes to fetch his camcorder.*

Alain   Without the video.

Pete *puts down his camcorder.*

Alain   I call this moment the End of History because what
we understood as history, this movement forward, has ended.
And the words which have for so long been our guides. . . .
Progress for example. This now means nothing.
We know this in our hearts. Every man, every woman, they
know it, they feel it, but they don't say it.
So we have to ask ourselves this question:
When will we embrace . . . (this is a word for you also,
embrace?)

Pete   Uh huh. Embrace. Yeah.

Alain   . . . chaos. When will we live the End of History?
When will we live in our own time?
And how will we live in this new age of chaos?
Not as we lived in the old age. Not with the old language. Not
by being more kind, more . . . enlightened.
We must be cruel, we must follow our desires and be cruel to
others, yes, but also we must be cruel to ourselves.
We must embrace suffering, we must embrace cruelty.

Pete   There's a lot to learn.

Scene Thirteen

Chorus   See, the Minister of our Church, he calls all the
moms together one day and he says:
'Ladies, we have to raise some money. We have to raise a lot
of money. Because I want the young people of this Church to
be part of the future, I want them to be on-line. We're going
to have a terminal and a modem right here for all our young
people so they can spread the word way into the future'.
And my mom and all the other moms worked real hard.
But when the terminal and the modem arrived they felt so
bad. Because their kids spent twenty-four-seven on the Net.
And one day they wake up and realise they are living in, like,
Valley of the Geeks and they never see their kids anymore.
And they go see the Minister. And there is wailing and, like,
the total gnashing of teeth. But he is just: 'Ladies, this is part

of the Lord's mystery. It may seem like he has taken your children away, but he is working for you in a mysterious way so let's get out there and raise those funds for more terminals and pray for a brighter world.'

Scene Fourteen

Pete *is on the Net, tapping at the keys.*

Enter **Alain**, *carrying brown paper bag.*

Pete   Where you been?

Alain   Walking.

Pete   You careful?

Alain   Oh yes. Very careful.

Pete   I don't like you to go out, but you go out, you be careful. They're out there.
You remember: this one is for Bill.

Alain   Of course I remember.
You wanna eat?

Pete   You shopped at a store?

Alain   Yes. A brown bag, like in the movies.

Pete   There is no need to shop at the store.
The store is a risk you don't have to take when we have a phone, we have a channel for groceries, a channel for meals . . .

Alain   I wanted to go to the store.

Pete   You go in a store, they have cameras watching you.

Alain   You gonna eat anything?

Pete   I'm not hungry right now.

Alain   What do you do on this?

Pete   I communicate.

Alain   Who do you communicate with?

Pete   Guys, mostly.
This way you get to know people, get to know people, like, really, really well but they don't know who you are.

Alain   Show me.

Pete   This is my space.

Alain   But I want you to show me.

Pete   Okay. For a while.
It's, like . . . my own home page.

Pete *taps onto a keyboard.*

Set it up just a few days ago and now there's like hundreds of subscribers.
See . . . Coming up now . . .

An image of a teenage boy, **Donny**, *on a computer screen.*

Donny   Hi, my name's Donny. How ya doing?
I've been really working on this. I want you to know that I really used to hate my body. I used to feel so uncomfortable, so ugly. But now I'm real happy with what I achieved. I've been working. And I tell you: you take the pain, you get the gain.

Donny *starts to remove his shirt.*

Pete   This guy's new.

Donny *reveals a torso that has been carefully scarred with a blade.*

Donny   Yeah. Look at these beauties. Look at that. Did it all myself. So come on, guys, you got anything better to show? I love these beauties, loves these little babies and I'm feeling so good. Feeling so good/ about myself.

Pete   No. I don't . . . I don't believe this.
Fuck you, Donny. Fuck you asshole. Fuck. Fuck.
Look at this guy. It's not for real.

Alain   He seems real.

Pete   No, no, no. Look, look, look.

Pete *uses the keyboard to enlarge the image.*

Pete See? See? Fucking ... ketchup ... fucking ... stagey fucking. Just some fucking actress, Donny, huh? Just some fucking fake. Fuck you.

Pete *turns off the image. He sobs.*

Alain No. Please. You mustn't ...

Pete I hate that. That really gets to me.

Alain It's just a game, yes?

Pete So many of them. Just because it's virtual. Doesn't mean you can lie, you know? Just because no one can reach out and touch it, doesn't mean you can fake it.

Alain He's just a little boy.

Pete This is supposed to be real.

Alain Of course.

Pete Everything's a fucking lie, you know? The food, the TV, the, the music ... it's all pretend. And this is supposed to be the one thing, one thing that's for real. Like you feel it, you mean it.
Like suffering, like cruelty.
I have to tell him. I'm gonna tell him.

Pete *types and* **Donny** *types his responses.*

Pete <DONNY, YOU ARE A FUCKING ACTRESS. YOU THERE DONNY?>

Donny <SURE, I'M HERE.>

Pete <DONNY, SO MANY OF THE GUYS ON THE PAGE ARE FAKES. IT'S NOT CLEVER OR FUNNY. IT'S EASY.>

Donny <I'M NO FAKE. I'M FOR REAL.>

Pete <NO WAY, GUY.>

Donny <WAY GUY. ALL THIS IS FOR REAL.>

Pete <GO FUCK YOURSELF DONNY.>

Donny   < MEET IF YOU LIKE. MEET YOU AND
YOU'LL SEE IF IT'S REAL. >

Pete   Well, how about that?
This guy wants to meet.
What do you think?
Let's get that fucking fake out here and let him see some
reality.
Alright then, yeah.
< OKAY, FELLA. LET'S MEET AND COMPARE OUR
CUTS. >

Alain   You do this also? Also you do this cuts to yourself?

Pete *removes his shirt. His chest is covered in cuts.*

Pete   See? I did it. I did it just like you said. Like suffering,
like cruelty.
You wanna meet him?
Let's meet him.

Scene Fifteen

Chorus   My name is Donny and I cut myself.
I had a big smile when I was a kid and my tongue was always
red and my lips were always red and my teeth were always
red. That was on account of my mom.
See, she worked nights in the store and so I'd go there after
school, hang out with my mom 'til, like, six in the morning
and every hour or so she'd say:
Donny, you want something?
Yes mom. I'm thirsty.
What you want, Donny?
Want a slushie, mommy.
Well, you help yourself, Donny, you go right ahead and you
take whatever you want.
And I'd go right up to the slushie machine, press that
cardboard cup in the hole . . . and I always had cherry.
Never even gave anything else a try, because it was
always cherry I wanted. Wasn't so much as curious about

the other choices.

So, six, seven, eight cherry slushies every night your teeth and your tongue and your mouth get pretty red.

Got so some guys called me Red Mouth Donny and some guys who didn't know me so well just called me Red. Which I liked.

Then, one day, the slushie machine was taken away. Some guy from the company just took it away. I think maybe the owner of the store hadn't kept up the payments, but he wasn't letting on.

And I felt so bad and no one could tell me why and by this time I wasn't a kid anymore, I was like eleven, twelve years of age, but that hit me so bad.

And I started to cuss the teachers and the cussing led to fighting with the teachers and that's when momma said she couldn't cope with me anymore and I had to move away from her.

Saw her a few times at the hospital because they wanted to study us on account of some professor who had a theory that it was something in all those slushies that made me angry with the teachers and something in the fluorescent light in the store that gave momma her cancer.

I reckon that's not true and those things just happened to us and that maybe if I get to ask Jesus one day he'll let me know. Jesus had quite a few cuts too by the end and I reckon he understands why I do this to myself.

I like Jesus, although I never met him. But I believe it's possible.

Scene Sixteen

Alain *and* **Pete** *are sitting in the dark.*

Alain   Of course, as we look back it will become easier to name the exact date.

Or we may never be able to say exactly. Perhaps we will never agree a fixed point. A moment.

There will be different theories.
/ But in principle we will agree.

Pete   Quiet, please. I need some quiet.

Alain   At some point, at a moment at the end of the
twentieth century, reality ended.
Reality finished and simulation began.

Pete   Jesus. Will you . . .?
Anyone ever tell you you talk too much?

Pause.

Alain   For myself, I would suggest fifteen hundred hours on
the thirteenth of August 1987.
Others may offer their own alternatives. A few hours, a few
days either side. So be it.
But there is a line, a divide and at some point (let's take my
point, fifteen/ hundred hours, August thirteenth 1987 as a
working model) at this point, although few of us noticed, or
sensed that the change was taking place, it happened.

Pete   No. Stop.
Stop now.
Why do you have to?
Oh yeah . . . blah blah blah.

Alain   Reality died. It ended.
And we began to live this dream, this lie, this new simulated
existence.

Pete   Reality just arrived.

Pete *presses play on the video. We see footage of* **Donny**'*s dead body,
covered in blood.*

Alain   Some examples?
Before, in the old world, there was an event, a moment,
which was followed by analysis, by the writing of history. /
Event – analysis – history.

Pete   Look at it.

Alain   And now?
We analyse, we project, we predict – CNN, talk radio – we

anticipate an event before it takes place: the fall of a wall/ in Berlin, a war in the Gulf.

Pete Look at what I'm showing you.

Alain And the event itself is just a shadow, a reflection of our analysis.

Pete Look, just look at it.

They sit in silence watching **Donny**'*s death, possibly repeated on a loop.*

Pete See?
This happened. We were there. It was real.
This isn't eyeballs in a shoe-box. The Japanese cannibal. There's no ketchup.
This is Donny.
Donny is dead. Donny is in there (*the kitchen*) and Donny is dead.
Did you think this was gonna happen?
Did you know?
You had any idea, it was your duty to jump in there, to intervene.
Why didn't you intervene?
He didn't have the experience, I guess.
Because if he'd use the home page a few times . . . If he'd just read the advice. Chest, legs, stomach are fine. If you wanna do a vein, then always cut across rather than up and seek medical assistance immediately afterwards. And don't ever do the jugular.
He should have known that.
He shouldn't have gone for the jugular.
I guess he was just so keen to prove that he was for real, you know?

Alain What we gonna do with him?

Pete Jeez, I dunno.

Alain Donny's gonna rot, he's gonna smell.

Pete A person, you know, there is so much.
So much skin and bone.

And brains and eyes.

What do you do with a person with no life in them?

I guess you bury them in the desert.

Chop them up, boil them but those guys always seem to get found out.

Hey, they have a whole crate of ice in the yard out there.

We fill the bath with ice and we put him in the bath until we figure out what we're gonna do.

(*To* **Donny**.) Donny, you're gonna be okay.

Donny, you're gonna chill.

(*To* **Alain**.) I haven't got this (*the disc*) and held onto it all this time for some . . . kid, who doesn't know how to use a blade fuck it all up for me, okay?

Scene Seventeen

Chorus   Donny knew. Donny knew what he was gonna do. Posted a message on the page before he headed out to these guys. Told those hundreds of subscribers:

'I'm heading out now for a real meeting. Had enough of just communicating with all you guys in a virtual kind of way. Had enough of it all just being pictures. See, some guys out there want me to make it real. So, I'm gonna meet them. Motel room and I'm gonna make it real. Totally real. I'm gonna go for my jugular.'

And you know something? He made every TV show, every talk show. Ricki and Oprah both got the same show: 'Death on the Net'.

And Stevie, he already has a song about it. Which he has performed unplugged and is now showing three times an hour on MTV.

Which seems to say to me that maybe Donny wasn't so pathetic after all, and he knew what was happening in his life and figured out a way to make something good from it.

Scene Eighteen

Motel room. Three days later. Empty.

Enter **Alain**. *Looks around.*

Enter **Pete**.

Pete   I sorted Donny out.

Alain   You got rid of Donny?

Pete   I got rid of Donny.

Alain   How did you do that?
How did you get rid of Donny?

Pete   Doesn't matter. Donny has gone, Donny has been
sorted out, okay?
We have to go.
I've packed.

Alain   Where do we have to go?

Pete   I don't know, someplace.
Just move on.
I've cleared our traces here.
Few more minutes and we're moving on.

Alain   You don't want to stay here.
You don't want to conceal yourself?

Pete   That's not possible anymore.
See, word is out. The word is out there.
They're all looking for us. They're checking each and every
motel in the State and we stay here, they're gonna find us.

Alain   You want to keep running?

Pete   That's right.

Alain   All the time, you just want to keep running?

Pete   That's the only thing to do.

Alain   You can't think of another possibility maybe?

Pete   There are no other possibilities.
Now, come on, move.

Alain   No.

Pete   Don't argue with me.
I don't need this.

Alain   We're not gonna run around like this.
I have the disc.

Pete   You have . . . ?

Alain   Last night, you were sleeping.
I got the disc.
I'm staying here.

Pete *produces a gun.*

Alain   I'm staying here.

Pete *approaches* **Alain**.

Alain   I'm staying here.

Pete   You come with me.
You give me the disc.

Alain   Who was cruel?
The Dutch woman or the Japanese man?
It was the woman, the woman was cruel.
Because she understood the use of metaphor and he
understood nothing.

Pete *shoots* **Alain**.

Alain *falls.*

Pete *retrieves the disc.*

Pete   I think that many people here would consider that
the Japanese guy was cruel.
Because he shot her. He ate her.
And I think that many people here would find that cruel.
And that blind woman see?
She would never have found that mailbox.

Exit **Pete**.

Scene Nineteen

Chorus   Looking back now I'm an adult, I think I used to cry at night not because the world was such a bad place.
Well, okay, not just because the world is such a bad place.
But also because I wanted the world to come to an end. Like Armageddon or Hellfire or Total Meltdown or somesuch catastrophe. And I cried because I felt so guilty because it was gonna happen any day and it would be all my fault for wanting it so much.
But the world hasn't ended. It's going on and on. And I keep on looking for signs that it's getting better like momma told me. But I can't see them.
So, it hasn't ended and it's not getting better. It's just going on, on and on and on.
And I wonder if I should feel something about that.
But – you want the truth? – I don't feel a thing.
See I'm the kind of person who can stand in the middle of an earthquake and I'm just like 'woah, neat earthquake'.
And I wonder what made me that way.

Scene Twenty

Hospital room.

Alain *is on a drip.* **Pete** *is reading from a piece of paper.*

Pete   Because Man is dead. For so many centuries, we have believed in his existence. This thing, this construct, this thing we called Man. But one day, some day in the twentieth century, he went and died. Sometime after Belsen, sometime after Kennedy, sometime after MTV, he went and died. As surely as, several hundred years ago now, God died and we trembled to live in a universe without him, so now we look around and see that Man is no more.
What do you think?

Alain   Well yes, this is . . .

Pete   Is it good?

Alain   Yes. This is fine.

Pete   Shall I carry on?

Alain   Please.

Pete   But now we see, we feel that we are no longer the subject, but the object of forces, we are a confusion, a collision of . . .

A beeping sound.

What is that?

Alain   It tells me to take my pills.

Pete   You wanna get them?

Alain   No.

Pete   Okay.
So we're . . . there's . . . okay, okay, I got it . . . so the question is: How will we live our lives? For just as surely as there was a great battle between the centuries-old myth of God and the newcomer Science, so the next millennium will see the fight between those who embrace and those who deny the death of man.
Would you say it's in any way derivative?

Alain   What would you say?

Pete   I've included examples of 'original thought'.

Alain   Then, fine.

Pete   For instance, well . . . for example, you make no references to MTV. I guess because you didn't have MTV when you wrote the book, right?

Alain   Exactly.

Pete   So that's an original thought, yes?

The beeping returns, louder and shriller.

Keeps on going doesn't it?
It's important you take your pills.

Alain   It's nothing.

Pete   I'm joining my dad.

He's taking me on as a sort of number two. We did a deal on the whole chaos disc thing.

Because, see I don't believe you.

Sure, I get your point. See, I can do the whole Death of Man speech thing, you know?

But where'd it get us?

It got us Donny.

And I don't want that anymore.

Pete *screws up the piece of paper.*

My dad built this house.

Well, hundreds of guys built this house out of my dad's . . . vision.

And in my father's house, his vision of the future, of perfection is realised.

Well, look, you own a painting, okay?

And that painting has a mood. But some days that may not be your mood and here is this painting mooding out the wrong mood down on you, you know?

But my dad has solved the problem.

He buys the exclusive rights to, like, hundreds of total masterpieces and then programmes them into walls and if your mood changes, click, whirr, the pictures change also.

And many, many other problems, he just went right ahead and solved.

I hate my dad.

But you offer despair, you know that? And it may be true, but it doesn't get us anywhere.

I'm sorry, I have a meeting to go to now.

I really want you to get better.

I really think you should take your pills.

Alain   I don't want the pills.

I don't want to get better.

Pete   Got you a present.

Pete *hands* **Alain** *a present in wrapping paper.*

To remind you of Donny.

See ya. Wouldn't wanna be ya.

Exit **Pete**.

Alain *opens the present.*
A shoe-box.
He opens the shoe-box.
Donny'*s eyes.*
The beeping gets louder and louder.